Why did ancient Greeks ride elephants into battle?

and other questions about the ANCIENT GREEKS

Tim Cooke

WAYLAND

www.waylandbooks.

First published in Great Britain in 2021
by Wayland

© Hodder and Stoughton, 2021

Credits:
Editor: Julia Bird
Design and illustrations: Matt Lilly
Cover design: Matt Lilly

ISBN hb 978 1 5263 1534 2
ISBN pb 978 1 5263 1535 9

Printed and bound in China

MIX
Paper from
responsible sources
FSC® C104740
FSC
www.fsc.org

Picture credits:

Alamy: Agefotostock 17c; Album 23; Falkensteinfoto 5,11c; funkyfood London-Paul Williams 4; Incamerastock 25bl; Lanmas 20c; North Wind Picture Archives 12c; Science History Images 11b, 26; The Print Collector 15t.
Shutterstock: Arka38 8; Josep Curto 12cl; Four Oaks front cover, 1, 14; Gilmanshin 7, 9b; Antonio Gravante 9c; Constantinos Iliopoulos 22; Jekatarinka 25br; Panos Karas 28tl; Derick D Miller 6b; Dima Moroz 17cr, 21c; Morphart Creation 27; Optimarc 24t; Lefteris Papaulakis 15b, 28tr; Lev Paraskevopoulos 18-19b; Pecold 6c; Pink Floyd yilmaz Uslu 29b; Valeriya Repina 28tc; Dmitry Rukhlenko 13b; S-F 19t; Stefania Valvola 24b; Wondervisuals 17t.
Wikimedia Commons/CCA-SA 3.0 15c.

Every effort has been made to clear copyright.
Should there be any inadvertent omission, please apply
to the publisher for rectification

Wayland
An imprint of
Hachette Children's Group
Part of Hodder and Stoughton
Carmelite House
50 Victoria Embankment
London EC4Y 0DZ

An Hachette UK Company
www.hachette.co.uk
www.hachettechildrens.co.uk

Contents

Ancient Greece

The ancient Greek civilisation dominated the ancient world between the 8th century BCE and the 2nd century BCE, when it was conquered by the Romans. Even under Roman rule, Greek culture still dominated much of the ancient world.

Mainland and islands

Greece has two main parts. The mainland is often rocky and mountainous, with a long coastline, while hundreds of islands dot the Aegean Sea. They range from the largest island, Crete, to tiny outcrops.

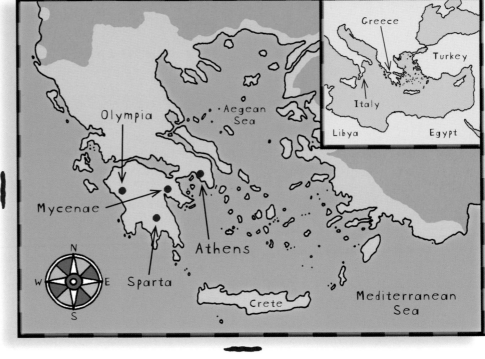

Boom and bust

Crete was home to the first Greek civilisation. The Minoans emerged there in around 2600 BCE. Their sailors voyaged and traded as far away as Egypt and Turkey. On the mainland, the warlike Mycenae reached a peak in about 1600 BCE.

Both of these Bronze Age civilisations ended suddenly in around 1100 BCE. Minoan trade collapsed, perhaps because of a huge volcanic explosion in the Aegean. The Mycenaean cities, meanwhile, were destroyed by foreign invaders.

A Minoan pottery jar dating from around 2100 BCE.

Then a dark period followed in ancient Greek history that we know very little about, until ...

Separate, but united!

Around the 8th century BCE, Greece started to emerge from its Dark Ages. Settlements that were cut off from one another by mountains or sea developed separately into city states.

These city states often fought. But despite their differences, their citizens had much in common: the same language, the same gods and the same culture. When they needed to fight their enemies – mainly the mighty Persian Empire – the city states worked together.

 The Greeks defeated the Persians at the Battle of Salamis in 480 BCE.

Inspiring Athens

In particular, the city state of Athens grew wealthy through trade and warfare. This was part of the Classical Age, when Greek culture reached a peak. Athens became a centre of learning whose scholars still shape life today.

What did the ancient Greeks do for us?

Well, a lot. Like:

- democracy (a Greek word meaning 'power of the people')
- modern mathematics
- the Olympic games
- the jury system
- the marathon
- astronomy
- philosophy
- sculpture.

An Olympic javelin thrower

When the Romans took power in Greece in 146 BCE, they borrowed many Greek ideas. Thanks to the Romans, these were passed on throughout Europe.

✳ Read on to find out more about the fascinating – and sometimes frightening – ancient Greeks ... ✳

Why did Minoans have strong ankles?

To somersault over charging bulls – obviously! That might seem a strange pastime (not to mention *VERY* dangerous). For the Minoans of Crete, though, the bull was sacred. Leaping over bulls was a form of worship.

YOUR ANKLES ARE LOOKING ESPECIALLY FINE TODAY!

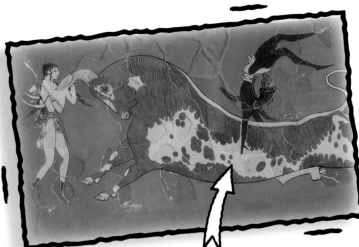

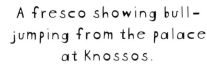

A fresco showing bull-jumping from the palace at Knossos.

Minos and the Minotaur

The Minoans were named after King Minos, who was said to be their first king. The royal palace at Knossos was decorated with frescoes of bulls.

LET ME OUT – I'M NICE REALLY!

Beneath the palace was a maze-like structure of small rooms. According to myth, this was the home of the Minotaur, a creature that was half-man and half-bull.

Mystery face

At about the same time as the Minoan civilisation emerged, mainland Greece was home to the Mycenaeans, who had grown powerful through war and trade.

In 1876, archaeologists explored the grave of a warrior from Mycenae. They found a lifelike mask made of gold. Experts thought this might be Agamemnon, King of Mycenae. He was said to have led Greek forces in a war against the city of Troy. In fact, we now know the mask is too old to show Agamemnon.

In which case ... who is it?

The mysterious Mycenaean mask

The Trojan War

Around the 700s BCE, the Greek poet Homer wrote *The Iliad*, a long poem about a war in which Greek warriors defeated the city of Troy. People thought the story was fiction until the ruins of Troy were discovered in the 1880s.

The poem describes how the ten-year siege of Troy ended when Greek warriors were smuggled inside the city in a wooden horse. The ruins showed that the city had been burned to the ground – just as Homer had described.

ARE WE THERE YET?

LOOK ... A HORSE!

Why did farmers beat their trees?

If you wanted to be a farmer, you probably wouldn't have chosen Greece: mountains, poor soil and rocky coastlines made it a difficult place to grow most crops. But one thing at least grew well there: the olive tree.

The olive tree looks a bit ... humble. It has a gnarly, twisted trunk and small silver leaves. But without it, there might never have been an ancient Greece.

WHO ARE YOU CALLING HUMBLE?!

Hard land, tough trees

Olive trees love sunshine, cool winters and poor soil, which makes Greece a perfect home. And their fruit is remarkable.

At harvest time, some farmers used long sticks to bash the branches so that ripe olives would fall to the ground, or into a net. Most farmers gently shook the trees to make the fruit fall without being bruised.

When is an olive not an olive?

Olives can be eaten as … well … olives, but they can also be pressed to make oil that has a lot of uses.

How many of these would you have guessed?

- as a dressing for salads
- as oil for cooking
- to burn for heating
- to burn for lighting
- as detergent for laundry

- to warm athletes' muscles
- as medicine
- as soap.

Olives were an important export. The Greeks traded their olive oil across the ancient world. They also grew grapes to turn into wine, which was the most popular drink.

CHEERS!

What's to eat?

The Greeks' most common farmed animals were sheep and goats. They provided milk and cheese, as well as meat (although the poor rarely ate meat). Many families kept hens, and there was plenty of fish from the sea. And if that all sounds like a modern menu, how about some locusts (fried in olive oil, of course) or black soup made from pigs' blood?

Could you start a city state in your bedroom?

Separated by mountains and often found on small islands, Greek communities developed separately. They became city states, which were made up of a city and the surrounding land that supported it with food and resources.

Big and small

There were more than 1,000 city states. Some were huge, like Sparta, or powerful, like Athens and Corinth. Others were no bigger than a small town. But no, none were quite as small as a bedroom.

Close, but not touching

Greece's geographical barriers meant that even close neighbours lived separately. They often had different laws and forms of government. Some were ruled by kings and others by councils of citizens.

Sparta vs Athens

This could lead to great differences.
Compare the two most powerful city states, Athens and Sparta:

Athens was ruled by an elected council. It had created an early system of democracy, or voting for political representatives. Athens was also a centre of art and learning. It was protected by a powerful navy.

Sparta, the second most powerful city state, was ruled by two kings and a council of elders. They weren't interested in democracy or the arts. They ruled Sparta as a military state. All the state's energies went into its army.

WHEN'S LUNCH?

Sparta's five ephors (leaders) were elected by the people to rule the city state.

Spartan soldiers (left) in action against the Persians at the Battle of Plataea in 479 BCE.

Greece united

In the face of a threat from outside Greece, the city states sometimes united to fight their shared enemy. In the 5th century BCE the massive Persian Empire invaded Greece twice. After the Persians took over most of Greece with a huge army, the city states joined together, led by the Spartan army and the Athenian navy, to fight back and finally defeat the Persians in 449 BCE.

Which city was inspired by an owl?

WELL, I AM VERY INSPIRING!

Athens became the richest and most powerful of all the Greek city states. Today, it is seen as the home of democracy, as well as a centre for the arts, philosophy and learning.

Athens ♥ Athena

Athens was named after the goddess of warfare and wisdom, Athena, whose symbol was the owl.

Owls have always had a reputation for being very wise. Perhaps it's because they have big eyes that make them look clever. The owl was stamped on the city's coins, and Athenian warriors painted it on their shields.

Athena

Owl

Athena's temple

Athenians believed that Athena protected them, so they built a temple called the Parthenon dedicated to her on the Acropolis (see page 13). Inside the temple stood a huge gold statue of the goddess.

The Parthenon was built after the Greeks defeated the Persian Empire in 449 BCE. The Athenian leader Pericles organised the rebuilding of the city, which the Persians had ruined.

Boys and girls ... and citizens

Education in Athens was very important. But only really for boys. Boys went to school to learn about poetry, drama, literature and sculpture.

Hooray!

Girls stayed home to learn about … running a home.

Boo!

Everyone learned how to be a good citizen. But who was a citizen?

Not just anyone. Only men could be citizens – and only if they had two Athenian parents. Women, foreigners and slaves were not citizens, so they had few rights – if any!

On the rocks

The Acropolis is a huge rocky outcrop that towers above Athens. Originally, it was a citadel where Athenians could shelter from attack. When Pericles rebuilt the city, he built a number of sacred temples there, including the Parthenon. Its gleaming marble could be seen for miles around.

Why did ancient Greeks ride elephants into battle?

CHARGE!

Well, why not? If you could go into battle on top of a charging elephant, wouldn't you? It probably felt a lot safer than marching into war!

Epirus's elephants

The Greek city state of Epirus got the idea of using war elephants from the Persians, who themselves had borrowed it from the Indians (who had lots of elephants).

Epirus borrowed 20 African elephants from Egypt, and in 280 BCE used them to defeat a Roman army. The Roman soldiers were terrified. Next time, however, they were ready. They used balls of fire to scare the elephants.

Soldier boys

Ordinary Greek soldiers, or hoplites, fought on foot. They wore bronze helmets and a bronze or leather breastplate, and fought in a formation called a phalanx. They lined up side-by-side, and each locked his round shield over that of his neighbour. That created a kind of wall as they advanced with their spears and swords in hand.

Hoplite

Awesome oar power

The Greek were also skilled at naval warfare. Their long warships, called triremes, were powered by many rowers.

☆ At the front, they had a bronze ram at water level that could punch a hole in an enemy ship to sink it.

Triremes also carried soldiers who were trained to leap onto enemy ships.

Strength of the Spartans

Sparta, the largest city state, was set up to produce tough warriors. At the age of seven, boys were taken from their parents and trained to be soldiers. The Spartans believed the best way to toughen up the young was to make life hard. Today, the word spartan is still used to describe a lifestyle with no comforts.

Statue of a hoplite known as Leonidas found in the ruins of ancient Sparta

Why did the Greeks work out naked?

The Greeks invented many modern sports, including running, javelin and wrestling. But they didn't invent any sports kit. Greek athletes competed naked. That might be one reason why married women weren't allowed to be spectators! (Women weren't allowed to compete, either.)

NO LOOKING!

Show yourself!

Sport wasn't just fun for the ancient Greeks. It was seen as a matter of life or death. Sometimes literally, because sport helped men become better warriors (especially in Sparta).

It was also a way to honour the gods by showing off the perfect human body. Athletes even covered their skin in olive oil to make it shine.

Olympic Games

The most important sports festival was the Olympic Games, held in honour of Zeus, the king of the gods (see pages 18–19). The first recorded Games were held in 776 BCE in Olympia (where the name comes from).

Olympia

The Olympic Games took place every four years from then on. They became so important that wars were halted to allow athletes to travel to Olympia. The winners, who were awarded a crown made from olive leaves, became superstars.

Discus-throwing

War games

Most ancient Greek sports related to the skills warriors needed. Competitors boxed, ran and threw the discus and javelin. They jumped over obstacles and rode horses. They lifted weights made of stone and lead. They wrestled, but were forbidden to bite their opponent or gouge his eyes.

HEY! NO BITING REMEMBER?

CENSORED

The Marathon

According to legend, the Greek soldier Pheidippides fought in the Battle of Marathon in 490 BCE. Here, the Greeks beat a Persian army, saving Athens from attack. Pheidippides ran as fast as he could to Athens to report the good news. He then fell down dead. (Maybe he should have taken a couple of breaks.) The distance from Marathon to Athens is now the standard distance of a marathon: 26.2 miles (42 km).

Did Greek gods dress as tramps?

JUST OFF TO HAVE FUN WITH SOME HUMANS.

According to ancient Greek beliefs, the gods often wandered down to Earth. If you met a beggar, it was better to be kind to him: it might just be the god Zeus in disguise! The gods could be quick to punish people who treated them badly.

Godlike gods

The Greeks believed they owed everything to the gods. And there were a lot of gods and goddesses. In fact, there were more than 400!

Holy mountain

To make life simpler, there were 12 main gods. These were the Olympians, named after Mount Olympus in northern Greece, where they were said to live. The peak of the mountain was often shrouded in mist, keeping the gods hidden away.

Hera
Queen of the gods

Aphrodite
Goddess of love

Apollo
God of music and prophecy

Artemis
Goddess of the moon

Hestia
Goddess of the home

Mount Olympus

Half and half

When they came down from Mount Olympus, the gods looked just like me or you. (Well, maybe a bit more godlike!) They had children with humans, who were demigods, such as the hero and warrior Achilles.

Mixed messages

The Greeks kept the gods happy in various ways – and especially by building temples. Every city held festivals and games to honour the gods.

One of the most important temples was Apollo's temple at Delphi. Apollo was the god of prophecy, and his priestesses, or oracles, passed on messages from the god to people trying to learn their future. These pronouncements could be interpreted in different ways. That also meant they could never be proved wrong!

Hermes
Messenger of the gods

Athena
Goddess of wisdom

Poseidon
God of the sea

Hephaestus
God of fire

Ares
God of war

Hades
God of the underworld

Ladies

Where were all the ladies' loos?

To be honest, public toilets didn't really exist in ancient Greece. But there would have been very few for women because most people in the streets were men. A woman's place was strictly in the home.

Happy housewives?

Girls in ancient Greece were brought up to be good wives, mothers and housekeepers. Married by the time they were 14 years old, girls learned how to bring up their children and run their homes.

YAWN ...

If their husbands could afford it, women had slaves to cook and clean so they could spend their days spinning and weaving. (Which isn't that much of an improvement.)

No rights isn't right!

Women had virtually no power outside the home. They could not vote or own land. They had to obey the men in their lives, in this order:

● husband   ● father   ● brother   ● any other male relative.

Leading women

There were some exceptions. In Sparta, women were allowed to own land – and they could even drink wine. In Athens, women were allowed to go out to collect water from public fountains (in most places, this was a job for slaves). It gave them a chance to see their friends and catch up on gossip.

Very wealthy women sometimes learned to read and write. Sappho, for example, was a female poet who lived in the late 7th century BCE She wrote about women's lives.

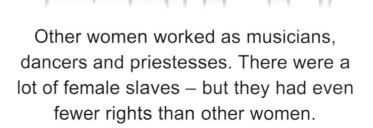

I'M JUST OFF TO COLLECT SOME MORE WATER.

AGAIN?!

Other women worked as musicians, dancers and priestesses. There were a lot of female slaves – but they had even fewer rights than other women.

Fun and games

Compared to Greek women, Greek men had all the fun. They held parties (known as *symposia*) where slave girls entertained the guests with dancing, acrobatics and flute playing. The men wore garlands of flowers and lay on sofas where they ate and drank wine as they discussed politics and philosophy – and inevitably fell asleep.

How did a broken vase help democracy?

Athens was not like most other city states. Well, for a couple of centuries, anyway. In the 5th and 4th centuries BCE, the Athenians ruled themselves. Athens is often seen as the world's first democracy.

Hill gatherings

A few times a month, citizens gathered on the Pnyx, a rocky hill on the Acropolis, to debate important issues. Anyone could speak on any issue, although 6,000 men had to be present for a debate to take place.

The Pnyx today

Let's take a vote

At the end of the debate there was a vote. Everyone's vote counted the same, and the majority won. There was no second vote! Most votes were decided by a show of hands.

On close votes, voters dropped a stone – **WHITE FOR YES**, **BLACK FOR NO** – into a large vase. When everyone had voted, the vase was smashed so the stones could be counted.

BLACK OR WHITE, HMM ...

Citizens' concerns spanned everything from deciding whether to go to war to making sure there was enough food. Although the assembly could approve laws, they couldn't create laws. That was done by a group of aristocrats, who held the real power in Athens.

Not quite democratic

If that sounds a lot like democracy today, it was … but. **A BIG BUT**. Not everyone could vote. Citizens were men over 18 years old who had been born in Athens. Women and slaves could not vote, and nor could anyone born outside Athens.

... And don't come back!

Occasionally, Athenians voted to banish someone from the city as a punishment. Voters scratched their decision on a piece of broken pottery called an *ostracon*. These ostraca give us the modern word 'ostracise', which means to exclude a person from society.

An ostracon vote for the banishing of an Athenian man called Themistocles

23

What was Pythagoras' theorem of beans?

The ancient Greek mathematician and philosopher Pythagoras is mainly famous today for his theorem about triangles. His theorem about beans is less famous for some reason!

$a^2 + b^2 = c^2$

NO BEANS FOR ME THANKS!

Disturbing the universe

Pythagoras advised against eating beans because they made the stomach gurgle. That didn't fit with his idea that humans should live in tranquillity and harmony, like the universe, which he believed was governed by the laws of mathematics.

A grumbling tummy was not a sign of perfect balance. Also, he thought that beans might have the same origins as human flesh. So eating them was like eating a person.

Ugh.

Think it through!

Pythagoras, who lived in the 6th century BCE, didn't accept lots of established ideas. He challenged the idea that the gods were behind what happened on Earth. Instead, he tried to explain the world through reason and mathematics.

Other ancient Greeks did the same. This new approach was called philosophy, which means 'love of wisdom'. (It's also called thinking very hard about very hard questions, like 'Why are we here?')

Deep thinkers

Western philosophy today was shaped by the ancient Greek philosopher Socrates in the 400s BCE. Though Socrates himself wrote nothing down, his pupil, Plato, wrote a book called *The Republic* about justice and government. It is still the most-read philosophy book of all time.

Plato set up a school, or academy, for philosophers in Athens. Its students included Aristotle, who studied everything from astronomy to poetry. Aristotle's most famous student became Alexander the Great, who conquered much of the ancient world.

Alexander the Great

Socrates

Plato

Pythagoras

Aristotle

This fresco of Plato's Academy was painted by the Italian artist Raphael (1483–1520).

Something doesn't sound right ...

Socrates was particularly interested in morality, or the difference between right and wrong. People were suspicious of the way he thought, however. He was found guilty of being hostile to democracy and sentenced to death. He died by drinking a cup of poison.

How did Archimedes defeat Rome with a magnifying glass?

The Romans who tried to capture the Greek port of Syracuse in 212 BCE hadn't counted on one thing. The city's defenders included one of the greatest scientists of all time: Archimedes.

Tall tales

The story goes that Archimedes designed a huge magnifying glass or mirror that focused the Sun's rays into a beam that set fire to the sails of the Roman ships. To be honest, it sounds doubtful.

Archimedes using the famous 'Archimedes heat ray' during the Battle of Syracuse.

Leave the mathematician alone!

Whatever the truth, Archimedes' defences helped the Greeks resist the attack for two years before they surrendered. The Roman commander issued orders that Archimedes should not be killed.

MEMORANDUM: WHATEVER YOU DO, DON'T KILL ARCHIMEDES

Archimedes was famous as the inventor of devices such as a screw that rotated to lift water from rivers and canals, so he could have been helpful to the Romans. Sadly, a Roman soldier killed him anyway. Maybe he didn't get the memo.

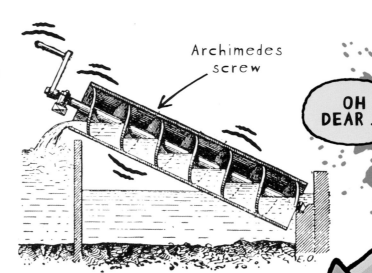

Archimedes screw

OH DEAR ...

Ancient Greece declines

The Romans eventually conquered the Greeks at the Battle of Corinth in 146 BCE. The Roman civilisation took over as the greatest power in Europe, but it remained heavily influenced by ancient Greek culture and philosophy, which has helped it to live on.

Hippocrates
Laid the foundations of modern medicine by basing treatment on observing his patients' symptoms.

☆ Science masters

Ancient Greek scientists made huge advances in science which help our understanding of it today. These are just a few of their discoveries:

Anaxagoras
Observed craters and mountains on the Moon, and realised that the planets moved.

Aristarchus
Figured out that Earth revolves around the Sun, which was finally proven to be true in the 1500s.

Thales of Miletus
Discovered Earth's solstices and equinoxes.

Democritus
Said the Milky Way is formed of thousands of stars.

Eratosthenes
Calculated Earth's circumference.

Galen
Greatly increased understanding of the body's circulatory and nervous systems.

Euclid
Said that light travels in waves or rays.

Claudius Ptolemy
Invented the science of optics, or vision.

Quick-fire questions

WE'RE ACTORS YOU KNOW!

How did Greek actors avoid their fans?

Actors wore masks while they were on stage, so no one could recognise them. Only men could act, and there were only three performers. They used masks so they could play different roles. A larger group of actors formed the chorus, which commented on the action to explain what was going on.

Why did the army need a trumpet player?

Greek hoplites fought in close formation, using shields for protection and long spears and short swords to attack the enemy. The hoplites' effectiveness depended on them all acting at the same time. A trumpet player marched with the army to mark time, so that the soldiers could coordinate their movements.

MY LIVER JUST SKIPPED A BEAT!

Why did Greeks feel love in their livers?

The ancient Greeks believed that the different organs of the body were each responsible for different things. They believed that emotions such as love were controlled by the liver (which actually helps us break down food and store energy). That might sound silly, but it's not really different from people today believing that love comes from the heart (which is actually just a pump for the blood). It was Hippocrates, who lived in the 400s BCE, who first showed that the human body was a single organism in which each part was related to all the others.

Why did Greek writing go in both directions?

The Greek alphabet developed around the 900s BCE and had 24 letters. It was written on various surfaces, such as wax tablets or a type of paper called papyrus, or carved into stone. Early Greek writing used a method called boustrophedon, in which alternate lines ran from left to right, as our writing does today, and then in reverse, from right to left! In these reverse lines, even the individual characters were reversed. That can't have been easy to read!

Glossary

Archaeologist Someone who studies the physical remains of the past.

Aristocrat Someone from a high-ranking family.

Banish To send someone away from a place as a punishment.

Circumference The distance around the outside of a circle.

Citadel A fortress standing above a city.

City state A city that governs itself and the nearby land.

Classical Relating to the high points of ancient Greek and Roman civilisation.

Democracy A system of government where people can choose their rulers.

Fortified Protected by walls against an attack.

Fresco A painting made directly onto a smooth wall.

Garland A ring made from flowers and leaves.

Gouge To stick one's fingers in someone's eyes.

Jury A group of people who decide the outcome of a legal trial.

Majority The larger of two groups of people.

Myth A story from the past which often featured gods and could be used to explain natural events, such as the seasons.

Oracle A priest or priestess who communicates messages from the gods.

Papyrus A paper-like substance made from the papyrus reed.

Philosophy The study of the nature of existence and knowledge.

Prophecy A prediction of what will happen in the future.

Resources Materials that have a helpful use.

Theorem An idea that can be proven to be true.

Trireme An ancient ship with three banks of rowers on either side.

Uninhabited A place where no one lives.

Mini timeline

776 BCE
The first recorded Olympic Games is held.

508 BCE
Athens becomes the first democracy.

480 BCE
The Greeks defeat the Persians in the Battle of Salamis. The Classical Age begins.

432 BCE
The Parthenon is built in Athens.

386 BCE
Plato founds the Academy in Athens.

146 BCE
Rome defeats the Greeks at the Battle of Corinth and conquers Greece.

Further reading

Websites

www.natgeokids.com/uk/discover/history/greece/10-facts-about-the-ancient-greeks/

This National Geographic page has a collection of facts about the ancient Greeks.

www.bbc.co.uk/bitesize/topics/z87tn39

This page has an index of articles and videos about the ancient Greeks on the BBC Bitzesize site.

www.dkfindout.com/us/history/ancient-greece/

This interactive map has information about ancient Greek society.

Books

Facts and Artefacts: Ancient Greece
by Tim Cooke (Franklin Watts, 2018)

The Genius of the Ancient Greeks
by Izzi Howell (Franklin Watts, 2020)

The History Detective Investigates: Ancient Greece
by Rachel Minay (Wayland, 2015)

Writing History: Ancient Greece
by Anita Ganeri (Franklin Watts, 2017)

Index